UNIQUE BRACELET PATTERNS

You've never Thought of Before

By
JA Steel

For those who love jewelry
and can't afford to buy it

And for Martha who
never wears bracelets.

Printed in the United States of America

First Printing, 2020

Drawn, written, published by J.A. Steel
All Sketches are original Design.
All Photos Original
All Designs Original

1. Three Strands
2. Crimp
3. Braid One color
4. Braid all three colors

1. Four strands
2. Over
3. Under
4. Over
5. Under
6. Repeat

5 Strands

Six Strands Simple

Try It another way

The End

I ran out of Ideas so this is the last page.... Stay tuned for more.

9 798600 770980